T0011804

Life Cycle of a Rabbit

by Meg Gaertner

FOCUS
READERS.

PIONEER

www.focusreaders.com

Focus Readers is distributed by North Star Editions:
sales@northstareditions.com | 888-417-0195

Produced for Focus Readers by Red Line Editorial.

Photographs ©: Shutterstock Images, cover, 1, 21 (arrows), 21 (adult), 21 (baby); iStockphoto, 4, 7, 10, 14, 17, 18; Dr. Keith Wheeler/Science Source, 9; Nature in Stock/Alamy, 13; Red Line Editorial, 21 (embryo)

Library of Congress Cataloging-in-Publication Data
Names: Gaertner, Meg, author
Title: Life cycle of a rabbit / by Meg Gaertner.
Description: Lake Elmo, MN : Focus Readers, [2022] | Series: Life
   cycles | Includes index. | Audience: Grades 2-3
Identifiers: LCCN 2021005876 (print) | LCCN 2021005877 (ebook) | ISBN
   9781644938317 (hardcover) | ISBN 9781644938775 (paperback) | ISBN
   9781644939239 (ebook) | ISBN 9781644939673 (pdf)
Subjects: LCSH: Rabbits--Life cycles--Juvenile literature.
Classification: LCC QL737.L32 G33 2022 (print) | LCC QL737.L32 (ebook) |
   DDC 599.32156--dc23
LC record available at https://lccn.loc.gov/2021005876
LC ebook record available at https://lccn.loc.gov/2021005877

Printed in the United States of America
Mankato, MN
082021

About the Author

Meg Gaertner enjoys reading, writing, dancing, and being outside. She lives in Minnesota.

Table of Contents

CHAPTER 1

Embryo 5

 **THAT'S AMAZING!**

Big Changes 8

CHAPTER 2

Baby 11

CHAPTER 3

Growing Up 15

CHAPTER 4

Adult 19

Focus on Rabbit Life Cycles • 22

Glossary • 23

To Learn More • 24

Index • 24

Embryo

Spring comes. Two rabbits **mate**. One is **male**. The other is **female**. The female rabbit will have babies. **Embryos** begin growing inside her.

Some mother rabbits dig holes in the ground. The holes are not deep. The mothers put grass and fur in the holes. They cover the holes with leaves.

Other mother rabbits dig **burrows**. The mothers will have their babies in either holes or burrows.

Big Changes

An embryo goes through many changes inside the mother. The embryo is tiny at first. But it quickly grows. New body parts form. The head forms. It has eyes, ears, and a mouth. Front and back legs form. The embryo grows for about one month. Then it is ready to be born.

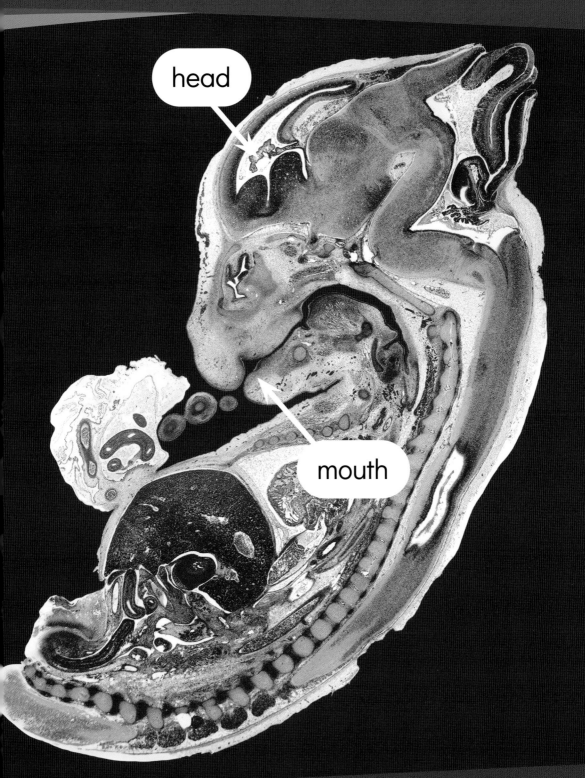

9

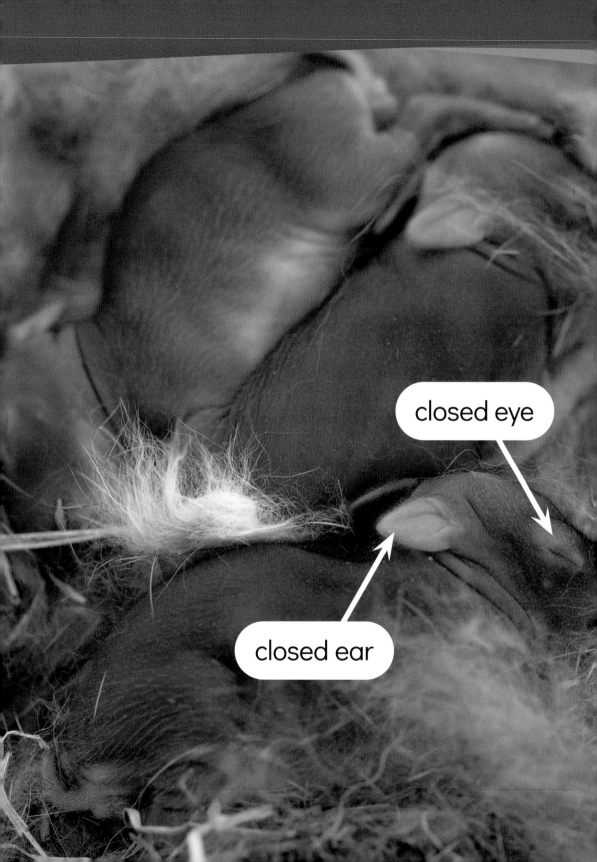

Chapter 2

Baby

The mother rabbit gives birth. She has several babies in one **litter**. The babies have no fur. Their eyes and ears are closed. They are **helpless** at first.

The mother leaves her babies each day. She eats food. Then she returns to the babies. The babies drink her milk. This milk has lots of **nutrients**. It helps the babies grow.

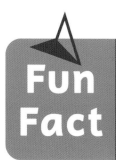

Fun Fact

A baby rabbit is called a kitten.

mother rabbit

baby

Chapter 3

Growing Up

Baby rabbits grow quickly.
Their eyes and ears open. They
grow fur. After a few weeks,
the babies stop drinking milk.
They eat plants instead. This
process is called weaning.

Soon, the young rabbits are ready. They leave their mother. They live on their own. The rabbits keep getting bigger. After a few months, they can have their own babies.

Fun Fact

A rabbit is an adult after one year.

Chapter 4

Adult

Adult rabbits have long
ears. They have short tails.
They have strong back legs.
This strength helps them
move quickly.

Soon, it is time to mate. A male and female rabbit come together. Embryos grow inside the female. The life cycle begins again.

Fun Fact A female rabbit can give birth to many litters during a year.

Life Cycle Stages

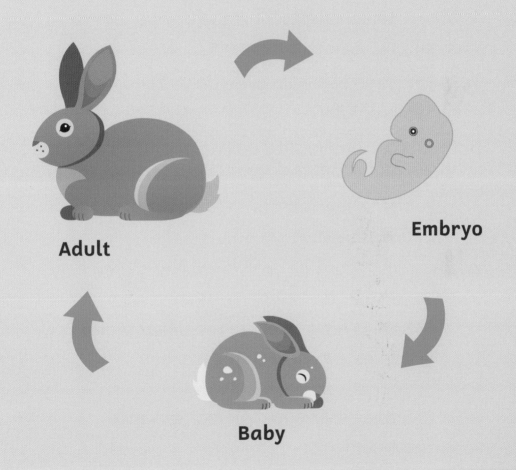

Adult

Embryo

Baby

Rabbit Life Cycles

Write your answers on a separate piece of paper.

1. Write a sentence describing what happens to an embryo inside its mother.

2. Which stage of the life cycle do you find most interesting? Why?

3. When can rabbits start having babies?
   - A. after one month
   - B. after a few months
   - C. after one year

4. Why can't babies leave their mother before they are weaned?
   - A. Babies have no fur to keep them warm.
   - B. Babies' eyes are closed, so they cannot see.
   - C. Babies still need their mother's milk for nutrients.

Answer key on page 24.

Glossary

burrows
Holes or tunnels that an animal digs to use as its home.

embryos
Animals in a stage of growth that happens before birth or hatching.

female
Able to have babies or lay eggs.

helpless
Unable to care for oneself or act without help.

litter
A group of babies born to a mother at one time.

male
Unable to have babies or lay eggs.

mate
To come together to make a baby.

nutrients
Things that people, animals, and plants need to stay healthy.

To Learn More

BOOKS

Boothroyd, Jennifer. *Meet a Baby Rabbit*. Minneapolis: Lerner Publications, 2017.

Geister-Jones, Sophie. *Rabbits*. Minneapolis: Abdo Publishing, 2020.

NOTE TO EDUCATORS

Visit **www.focusreaders.com** to find lesson plans, activities, links, and other resources related to this title.

Index

B
babies, 5–6, 11–12, 15–16, 21

E
embryos, 5, 8, 20–21

F
female, 5, 20

M
male, 5, 20

N
nutrients, 12

W
weaning, 15

Answer Key: **1.** Answers will vary; **2.** Answers will vary; **3.** B; **4.** C